Improving Healthcare & Retail Customer Experiences

Theresa M. Gargano-Adamski, MBA, MS

IMPROVING HEALTHCARE & RETAIL CUSTOMER EXPERIENCES

Theresa M. Gargano-Adamski, MBA, MS

To my parents, Vito J. Gargano and Theresa M. Gargano. I am abundantly grateful for their gifts of life and love, but most of all for instilling in me the mindset of expecting nothing but the best of myself and others.

CONTENTS

PREFACE

Healthcare and retail sectors share the same set of objectives, chief among them are customer care, brand building, revenue growth, customer retention and delivery of customer needs. To be successful, both sectors must recognize that their customers have choices. Whether they are shopping for a new physician or selecting a toaster, customers want their needs anticipated and satisfied in a simple, seamless, pain-free manner.

Healthcare and retail enterprises must walk in the customer's shoes and closely examine each touchpoint (or point of contact) that customers[*] will encounter along their journey when they purchase a product or service. For example, if a primary care physician refers a patient to an orthopedic surgeon, the patient

---

[*] *The word "customer" also refers to patient.*

will likely encounter the touchpoints below before even meeting with the surgeon for an "Establish Care" (first) appointment:

- Surgeon's website: Patient will determine his or her satisfaction with surgeon's credentials, board certification in practice specialty, hospital affiliations, experience, absence of disciplinary actions, insurance plan acceptance, in-network status, patient access to lab data, prescription refill procedure, patient reviews, awards, philosophy of care
- Call Center Agent: Patient will determine his or her degree of satisfaction for wait time on-hold, ease of scheduling appointment, office hours and policies
- Appointment Confirmation: Patient will determine if his or her appointment confirmation is delivered through their preferred method of communication

How familiar are you with the touchpoints that your customers encounter when interacting with you and your organization?

INTRODUCTION

This book offers you, as an organization leader, essential insights about the challenges shared by healthcare and retail sectors, and how the retail sector has addressed some of these challenges. You will also enhance your understanding of how a customer's journey in purchasing a product or service is impacted by touchpoints that retail and healthcare customers share. We will examine these questions:

- Can healthcare embrace and adopt retail strategies to help achieve more patient-centered care?
- How best can healthcare and retail sectors improve on their customer experience?
- Could laborious steps in customer journeys be identified and removed,

resulting in a simple, irritant-free experience?

We will examine some of the touchpoints shared by healthcare and retail customers along their journey in purchasing a product or service. These touchpoints include call centers, voice response systems, waiting lines, check-ins/check-outs, waiting areas, forms, staff and the web.

During the process of purchasing a healthcare product or service, your customers may encounter irritants that negatively impact their experience. These irritants are roadblocks to care, which we will discuss along with some ways to correct them. Healthcare irritants include:

- Discovering that a hospital gift shop is closed on Saturdays, Sundays and holidays though these are the days that most people visit patients

- Using the voice response system from a pharmacy to determine if a prescription is ready, only to hear the system say that the prescription was already picked up
- Guessing at a healthcare provider's office hours when the outgoing message says, "We are also open every other Saturday." Unless the recording specifies first and third Saturdays or second and fourth Saturdays, this recording is useless.
- Sitting in the waiting room of an orthopedic surgeon's clinic in a chair so low to the ground that it makes it difficult for a patient to rise from it
- Visiting a relative in a hospice setting, where the walls of her room are painted dark gray
- Completing an online "New Patient Form" in its entirety for the second time due to an input error made in only one field of the form
- Being given "New Patient Forms" to complete at a healthcare provider's office

and having to balance them on your lap
as you were not provided with a clipboard
- Reading the front page of a billing
statement that reads, "See Reverse
Side for Important Information" when
important information belongs on the
front page
- Being led to an exam room by a medical
assistant who is walking 20 feet ahead of
you, talking to the wall that she is facing,
and unaware that you can't hear her

Clearly, the above irritants detract from the
customer experience. Do you know where your
customers are likely to encounter irritants
during their journey? Do you know which
touchpoints are helping you to retain your
customers? How about the touchpoints that
are causing you to *lose* customers? Can you
identify them?

All businesses are customer-led, and
enlightened leaders recognize this. They

know that when detractors and irritants along the customers' journey are removed, their customers are more likely to return, and they tell others about their positive experience. Your efforts in developing and executing a simple, seamless, pain-free purchasing experience, be it healthcare or retail, will most likely be rewarded with increased revenue and satisfied, repeat customers who rave about your organization, your product and your service.

Your time is valuable. So before you read another page, you should know what this book is *not*. The pages that follow won't offer esoteric, pie-in-the-sky examples. Instead, they outline problem areas that interfere with an optimal customer experience, and practical, actionable improvements, in layman's terms, that offer quick wins for you as a leader and improved experiences for your customers.

1

THE HEALTHCARE LANDSCAPE – A PARADIGM SHIFT

IN THE PAST WE HAVE seen isolated healthcare services being offered in retail settings. Remember optical departments in Sears® stores? Contrast that with the present-day availability of 3D customer-printed orthotics at Costco®. Increasingly, healthcare is emerging in more nontraditional settings, making more of a brick-and-mortar footprint. Examples include:

- Target®
- CVS® MinuteClinics/CVS® acquisition of Aetna®
- Walmart® Care Clinics
- "Concierge" health services
- Walgreens® Healthcare Clinics

Historically, patient-physician relationships as well as healthcare settings have both been physician-centered and silo driven, as opposed to multidisciplinary, cohesive teams of practitioners that converge to care for the patient. Patient journeys are often fragmented between multiple providers. Consider the elderly patient in a hospital emergency room. She is alone, told to change into a hospital gown, transported to test after test, and confronted by strangers who are speaking in medical terminology.

Given the emerging technologies now available, and the growing emphasis on patient-centered care, isn't it realistic to expect that healthcare might soon meet the patient where *she* is, possibly in a more retail-based setting?

Lateef[1] refers to the coordination and integration of care, stating that patients feel vulnerable when they are faced with illnesses and they feel the need for competent and caring healthcare personnel. They need to make that "connection" and feel comfortable with all aspects of that care i.e. front line or acute care, auxiliary as well as support staff. The seamless patient and process flow will help with this objective and at the same time, enhance patient safety elements.

Remember, you can't improve what you do not measure. That's why healthcare and retail leaders must ask themselves:

1. What types of customer complaints have we received this week? Have they been added to the staff meeting agenda for resolution?

2. Who is assigned to monitor customer calls?
3. Who has contacted our Call Center posing as a customer so that we can evaluate the appropriateness of complaint resolution?
4. How can we best retain our current customers?

Whether a customer is having her teeth cleaned, opening a bank account, returning a pair of shoes or scheduling a colonoscopy, she expects that those responsible for delivering her customer experience have identified and simplified each step in her journey. She expects that her irritants have been strategically anticipated and tactically removed. But what if they haven't?

If they haven't, leaders in both healthcare and retail may never know because most dissatisfied customers will not tell you about their dissatisfaction. They simply will not return to your store or medical office. Moreover, they will tell others about their experience. Think about it. On those occasions when you are a dissatisfied customer, aren't *you* more likely to share your experience with others than when you are satisfied?

In fact, as Daniel Newman explains in his article in *Forbes*,[2] consumers tell an average of nine people about a positive experience with a brand, but they will tell 16 people about a negative experience. This book, and specifically the improvements that I believe are essential to a positive customer experience, grew out of a passion for expecting superb service for myself and those I care about.

For as long as I can remember, I've been the one that friends and family have turned to with heightened frequency for resolution of their consumer issues. When asked, "What do you do better than anyone else in the world?" My answer always was and still is a confident, "I complain effectively." I've cited a few examples below:

I'm one of those people who will walk into a doctor's office or retail store and immediately summon the manager to inquire, "Would you have someone move the planter that's positioned near the door? It's blocking customers with walkers and they may fall."

I've been known to enter a hospital lobby, encounter a confusing sign, and explain to the woman at the Information Desk why it should be worded differently. "Your sign is being read by people who are seeing it for the first time. Because you work here and you are familiar with the context, you understand it but visitors probably won't."

I was in the liquor department of a grocery store, shopping for a bottle of wine and a corkscrew to give as a hostess gift. I asked the clerk where the corkscrews were. He said that corkscrews weren't sold in the liquor department and they could be found elsewhere in the store. I asked the store manager why this was so, as it required me to walk to the opposite end of the store. I also asked, "If you display bottles of tartar sauce near the seafood, then why aren't corkscrews sold in the liquor department?"

Get the idea? To me, things must make sense. When they don't, I ask "Why?" Therein lies the impetus for this book. I don't accept situations that are beneath my expectations. I want the best for myself and those I care about. As a leader in your organization, you should aim for the very best for your customers.

In this era of social media, when one negative encounter can equal bad publicity, can you afford to overlook any options to make your customer experience best in class? Don't you wish that you had an opportunity to transform negative experiences into positive ones? You do! Read on.

Healthcare is just beginning to discover what the retail sector has always known. That to deliver best in class customer experiences, organizations must:

- Connect with customers;
- Identify and understand the customer journey; and
- Anticipate and deliver what matters to customers.

To connect with customers, enlightened managers engage their customers by listening to them, personalizing their experiences, and assisting them both during and after the product or service selection process. They view the customer experience as long-term strategic rather than short-term tactical. In short, they practice relationship retailing, a strategy that builds loyalty and long-term relationships with customers.

In their efforts to identify and understand the customer journey, successful managers map out the touchpoints representing each interaction that the customer has with their organization before, during and after they purchase a product or service. Touchpoints should be monitored at both the macro and micro areas of the customer's journey and examined for flow, functionality and effectiveness. Ask yourself:

1. When did I last step into my customer's shoes to map out their touchpoints?
2. When is the last time I walked through my customer's brick-and-click journey to discover what they experience both in-store and online?

Examples of touchpoints include:

- Advertising
- Annual wellness exam
- Assembly instructions
- Billing
- Call Centers
- Checkout lines

- Contact forms
- Coupons
- Customer Service
- Delivery of an appliance
- Insurance claims
- Interactive voice response systems
- Kiosks
- Live chats
- Marketing materials
- Mortgage applications
- Online Help Centers/Service Departments/Customer Service Desks
- Packaging
- Pharmacies
- Preparation instructions for a frozen dinner
- Product inserts
- Product returns
- Refunds
- Social media
- Surveys
- Technical support
- Trade shows

- Websites
- Wellness check by a visiting nurse

As you reviewed the above list of touchpoints, did you identify the ones in your organization that may be causing you to lose customers? How about the ones that are helping you to *retain* them?

As you proceed to anticipate and deliver what matters most to your customers, remember that the more you know about your customers and their needs, the easier it is to fulfill those needs.

Listen to your customers and rely on the tools that collect, prioritize and deliver customer data. These tools will facilitate a more robust and customer-centric approach to connecting with them. As a result, you will demonstrate to your customers that you care about what they care about.

The feedback that you receive will help you discover the roadblocks that prevent superior customer experiences. Do the roadblocks listed below prevent you from connecting and communicating with *your* customers?

- Signage (non-existent or unclear)
- Patient comfort (Would you ask your arthritic mother, cane in tow, to walk down a hall that's a block long to get to her exam room?)
- Interactive voice response systems at pharmacies that inform customers that their prescriptions had already been picked up when the customer calls to discover if it is ready for pickup
- Repeating identification information and account numbers to all three of the customer service agents one is transferred to
- Purchasing a gift card for home improvement store A at any grocer, drug store or retailer but only being able to purchase a gift card for home improvement store B at home

improvement store B, which requires a
special trip
- Discovering that a hospital gift shop is
  closed on Saturdays or Sundays when
  these are the days that most people visit
  patients
- Calling your store after hours, only
  to have the outgoing recording invite
  customers to call back during "business
  hours" when the recording does not
  specify what those hours are
- Making customers guess at healthcare
  provider availability when office hours
  are given in an outgoing recording,
  such as: "We are open every other
  Saturday." Is that *this* Saturday (first
  and third Saturdays of the month)
  or *next* Saturday (second and fourth
  Saturdays)?
- Being in the checkout line at a grocery
  store, asking to purchase a book of stamps,
  and being told to go to Customer Service,
  requiring you to wait in yet another line

- Toy departments and toy stores not enlisting a senior citizen "elf" who can relate to and assist grandparents in finding the toys their grandchildren ask for
- Telephone solicitor recordings that direct you to the company's website to be placed on a 'Do Not Call' list when you are 90 years old and don't own a computer. Shouldn't it be as easy as pressing 1 on the phone?
- Completing an entire online form all over again if you make a mistake in only one field
- Visiting a website to inquire about a product, and being asked to complete a Contact Form so that someone can research your question and respond to you. Chances are you'll migrate to a competitor's site so that your question can be answered *now* via live chat.
- Organizations that do not identify themselves by clearly displaying their

> business name and number on caller ID
> systems
> - Receiving treatment at an urgent care
>   facility, paying the bill, and reviewing the
>   receipt that reads, "We appreciate your
>   business! See you soon!"

It may be that one or two aspects of a customer's experience were hassle-free, but the rest of it was full of irritants. Managers must remember that it is the entire journey, not the individual touchpoints that comprise the quality of a customers' overall experience and determine if they will continue or discontinue purchasing from your organization. A study from Bain & Co.[3] shows that while 80% of the 362 firms surveyed believe they deliver a "superior experience," in contrast, when asked, customers say only 8% are really delivering.[3]

When detractors and irritants along the customer's journey are removed, customers are more likely to return. Your investment in developing and executing a seamless purchasing experience will most likely be offset by increased revenue from satisfied, repeat customers.

2

THE CALL CENTER

To the customer, a Call Center is the person at the other end of the phone when you call any organization. It is the voice of your company, hospital, clinic, or home health agency. The call center has the potential to be a profit center or a cost center.

What makes a good call center? In The Effortless Experience, Matthew Dixon, Nick Toman and Rick Delisi[4] explain that enlightened, low-effort companies have moved away from the "stopwatch" and "checklist" culture that has long permeated the service organization to instead give agents more autonomy and the opportunity to exercise a greater degree of judgment.[4]

You may have decided to outsource your organization's Call Center for financial and other reasons. If your company is still deciding on whether or not to outsource, consider these factors:

1. Can our organization effectively evaluate the data that our call center will generate?
2. Can we absorb the cost of call center equipment including appropriate software platforms?
3. Are we able to hire, train and retain qualified call center staff?
4. Do we need a call center that is operational 24/7? If yes, are we appropriately staffed to absorb this function?
5. Can we identify call center organizations that handle companies similar in size and scale to ours?

Call centers exist to assist the customer and provide the organization with a platform from which to build their brand.

Outsourcing may provide your organization with economies of scale, international reach, a dedicated staff to handle calls, and technological applications that are aligned with yours. Remember however, that when you outsource your call center you are placing your brand in someone else's hands.

Before I describe some hypothetical Call Center scenarios, I want to stress the importance of respecting the customer's time. This means recognizing when the issue has been resolved to the customer's satisfaction, clarifying that no further action is required, and ending the call courteously and promptly with a brief, "I'm glad that I could help. Is there anything else I can do for you? No? Then thank you for banking with us. Goodbye." Instead, some agents, no doubt in an effort to be friendly, have separation anxiety and offer several marketing-related "closing statements" that keep the customer on the phone, wasting their time. Here are some examples of such statements from a typical banking institution Call Center agent:

- "Remember, we're open 24/7 online."
- "Let us know if we can assist you with anything else."
- "May I tell you about our no-fee checking account?"
- "Do you need a larger safe deposit box?"
- "We love young savers. Did you know that we offer savings accounts for children at no cost?"

You get the idea. Call Center agents should respect the customer's time. Below you will find a few less-than-positive Call Center customer experiences. As you read them, ask yourself if your organization is guilty of causing these same irritants among your customers.

HYPOTHETICAL CALL CENTER SCENARIO #1

Imagine that a patient has a Computer Tomography (CT) scan and asked the technician when the results would be sent to their physician. After being told that the results would be ready in 24 hours and not having heard from his physician in 48 hours, he called what he thought was the physician's office, but had actually reached the Call Center. He told the agent that he wanted the CT scan results and the interpretation.

The agent said that the doctor had left for the day. The patient left a message requesting the results and the report.

When he did not hear from the physician the next day (a full 72 hours from the expected time), he drove to his physician's office to get the information he needed. He was told that the physician had left the office, and so he asked to speak with a nurse. He waited 90 minutes to do so. Finally a nurse came into the waiting room to speak with him. "You must call next time," she said. "We're very busy." He asked, "Is doctor still seeing patients today? I was told by the Call Center that he had left for the day."

Anyway, when he asked for the CT scan results, the nurse replied, "If doctor thought that the scan results presented an emergency he would have called."

He told the nurse that her response was unacceptable and once again asked for the information. The nurse gave him a copy of the report which was full of medical jargon. He left the building, got into his car, and sobbed. "Requesting and receiving vital health information should not hurt," he said to himself. Then he pulled himself together and with the assistance of the expert research librarians at a public library who had a working relationship with a medical library, he was able to understand the findings of the report. He felt empowered.

A few weeks later, after he interviewed new physicians, he settled on a fabulous choice. He then fired the original physician.

Questions for Hypothetical Call Center Scenario #1:

1. Did the Call Center or nurse represent the physician effectively?
2. How well is your Call Center representing you, your store, your practice, your hospital?
3. Knowing that you can only improve what you measure, have you taken the 'temperature' of your Call Center? What data do you have?
4. When is the last time that you posed as a customer or patient, called your own Call Center and witnessed for yourself how your customers are being treated?
5. At team meetings within your store or clinic, is "Customer Complaints" an agenda item?

6. Have you considered the possibility of potential negative reviews from your patient's caregivers or loved ones?
7. Have you considered the impact that Call Center agents and medical staff can have on your practice?

How could the situation in Hypothetical Call Center Scenario #1 be improved upon? Could the Call Center agent have double-checked with the doctor's office to see if he was actually in the office? Yes. Could the nurse have put him at ease? Certainly. She could have offered to send the CT scan results to the physician's phone for him to review and interpret on the patient's behalf. She could have contacted the radiologist that wrote the report, and asked for a layman's interpretation. She did neither. The former patient will never forget what happened. And yes, he told everyone he knew about his experience.

HYPOTHETICAL CALL CENTER SCENARIO #2

Imagine that your friend purchased a set of four kitchen chairs from a home improvement store. Soon after they were delivered and assembled, she sat on one. It broke. She called the store where she had purchased the chairs. The Call Center agent presented her with two choices.

Choice A: Bring all four chairs to the store using her time, her gas, and her compact sedan. As the chairs were already assembled, her compact sedan dictated that she would need to make two trips to return the chairs.

Choice B: The store would arrange for a shipper to pick up the chairs from her home within three days (no specific day or time window was offered). She asked the agent, "What if I'm not home when the shipper arrives?" She was told that she could leave the chairs outside. She thought, "Leave the chairs outside subject to theft and the weather?" That didn't make sense to her.

Neither choice was acceptable to her but she chose Choice A and returned the chairs to the store so that she could receive an immediate refund. After all. She was doubtful that after this incident she would purchase another set of chairs from this home improvement store, and she wanted her money back. While in the store, at the Customer Service desk, she told the team member what had happened, as well as the options that were given to her by the Call Center agent. She asked the team member, "Would you offer those choices to your mother?" The team member said that this was the store's policy. Clearly, she had not been empowered to use her best judgment. How could this scenario be improved?

The Call Center agent should have called her back within 24 hours with some date and time windows. Her store manager should pick up the chairs at her home using the store van, and he should issue her a refund on the spot, along with their apologies and a gift card to use in the store so that she can select a new set of chairs.

The above example demonstrates the importance of test-driving your organization's policies with people that you trust. Would your mother stand for them? Do your policies have elasticity or are they unnecessarily rigid? Are you asking your customer-facing employees to stand behind a policy that they wouldn't accept themselves?

HYPOTHETICAL CALL CENTER SCENARIO #3

Imagine that a potential customer called a retail electronics store to ask if they sold transistor radios. The phone prompts assume that the customer has already placed an order. There is no prompt that matches her question. The menu repeats. And repeats. The customer is forced to listen to it and she hopes that after listening to the menu three times, a voice will tell her that she is being transferred to an agent. No such luck.

As a last resort, she presses the digit that corresponds to the prompt most likely to address her question. After an excruciating seven minutes on the phone with no results for the customer and no sale for the retailer, a human answers the phone. The customer asks, "Do you sell transistor radios?" The agent asks her for the Stock Keeping Unit (SKU) number. "How would I know the SKU number for an item I don't have?" she asks. The agent looks up the item. The store doesn't carry it. There is no offer to contact other branches of the store to see if another store might have one. There is no apology. There is no "Have you tried calling _____?" What a waste of time for the customer. What a missed opportunity for the retailer. The customer believes that this experience is unacceptable, and proceeds to tell her friends, colleagues and relatives about it.

How could this scenario be improved on? Clearly lacking here is an appreciation for "potential" customers. Organization leaders must not assume that all phone calls are from current customers. They must ensure that the technologies and systems that are in place focus on customer inclusion, not exclusion.

HYPOTHETICAL CALL CENTER SCENARIO #4

Imagine calling your physician's office to ask if he or she is in and the receptionist asks, "What is the patient's name?" Would the patient be tempted to ask, "Why? Is he in for some patients and not for others?" This example points to the merits of Call Center agents going off script when appropriate, using their judgment, and simply answering the question that is being posed to them.

3

KEEP IT SIMPLE, KEEP IT STICKY

CUSTOMERS ARE OVERWHELMED WITH CHOICES. Somewhere along the line, it wasn't enough to enjoy (only) yellow mustard on hot dogs. Now, yellow mustard is but one of five common mustard varieties, the other four being Dijon, honey, whole grain and powdered. These varieties are further categorized into sub-varieties, such as wasabi mustard. No matter which variety customers select, they are presented (confronted?) with a dizzying array of options in the condiment aisle of their grocery store.

With all the time pressures that customers encounter, do they really want to choose between multiple varieties of mustard? The same thing goes for olive oil, vinegars and a host of other products. With this being the case for products like condiments, just imagine the overwhelming customer experience one may have when purchasing a television, sofa, or even cereal.

Think about a typical morning at breakfast. Children are bombarded with cereal choices, and their selection may be determined by an accompanying toy in the cereal box. Today's moms may offer several choices to their children, asking if they prefer oat squares plain or dusted with cinnamon, or if they are in the mood for corn squares or rice puffs. In sharp contrast, on any given morning, my mom would announce, "I'll have your oatmeal ready in a few minutes." As a product of the fifties, a simpler time, I was fortunate to have a wise

and loving mother who firmly believed that
simple, healthy habits need no embellishment.

It turns out that customers actually *prefer*
simple experiences. In her article, "Consumers
will spend more on simple brand experiences,"
Charlotte Rogers[5] reported that consumers
are prepared to spend 62% more for a simple
experience when they shop.[5]

Customers want simple, seamless experiences
so that they can spend more time enjoying
the products that they purchase. What does
"simple" mean? Quite simply, it is a stress-free
environment in which to make product choices.
Take a look at the homepage of Google® or
the "house brands" of Aldi® or the minimalist
design of Ikea®. These brands focus on solving
customer irritants, not creating them. What
is the most important quality that defines a
simple experience? Ease of purchase. Does
your organization make it easy for customers
to purchase your products and services?

Consider the Global Brand Simplicity Index[TM] [6].
The 2017 Global Brand Simplicity Index[TM] is
a report of global brand ratings, based on an
online survey of more than 14,000 customers
in nine countries who rated a total of 857
brands to gather perspectives on simplicity
and how industries and brands make people's
lives simpler or more complex. Among the key
findings were that 64 percent of consumers
are willing to pay more for simpler experiences.
In addition, a stock portfolio of the simplest
brands outperforms the major indexes by 330
percent.[6]

Spenner and Freeman, in their article, To
Keep Your Customers, Keep it Simple[7]
surveyed and interviewed more than 7,000
consumers to discover what makes customers
"sticky" – that is, likely to follow through
on an intended purchase, buy the product
repeatedly, and recommend it to others. They
looked at the impact of stickiness for more
than 40 variables including price, customers'

perceptions of a brand, and how often consumers interacted with the brand.

The single biggest driver of stickiness, by far, was "decision simplicity" – the ease with which consumers can gather trustworthy information about a product and confidently and efficiently weigh their purchase options.

It is a clear commitment to saving the customer time. Spenner and Freeman concluded that what customers want from marketers is, simply, simplicity.[7]

Place yourself in your customer's shoes and track their journey all the way through to their completed purchase. Can you identify and remove unnecessary processes, steps and roadblocks?

———•———

4

IMPROVEMENTS FOR HEALTHCARE

CAN A PHYSICIAN PROPERLY ASSESS a patient in 15 minutes? Unlikely, right? Yet that's the average length of an office visit today. These precious minutes should be spent listening to the patient and observing nonverbal cues, not hammering away at a keyboard. Only after achieving patient engagement and completing a patient assessment should information be entered into the patient's electronic medical record. Unfortunately, during appointments, most physicians look up from their laptops only to ask a question. This is not conducive to patient engagement or a foundation of trust.

Consider the hypothetical healthcare scenario below that cries out for urgent care.

Hypothetical Healthcare Scenario

Imagine a customer waiting in line at the pharmacy with his hard copy prescription. In front of him, pharmacy technicians are in partitioned sections and above them is a sign that reads, 'Pickup.' There is no 'Drop Off' window. The only other window has a 'Consultation' sign above it. He is clearly dropping off a prescription. He proceeds to the Consultation window thinking that someone will attend to him.

The pharmacist approaches the Consultation window and directs him to get back in line to wait for a pharmacy technician who will 'triage' him. A simple edit to the sign such as 'Pickup/Drop Off' would have prevented

this needless waste of time for the customer.
Equally troublesome is the pharmacists'
use of the word 'triage' with a customer.
The customer may have known its' meaning
but most would not. According to Merriam-
Webster,[8] triage is "the sorting of patients
(as in an emergency room) according to the
urgency of their need for care." Remember,
language should *include*, not exclude.

How could this hypothetical scenario be
improved upon? The pharmacist should have
said, "I don't want to send you back in line. I'll
take care of filling your prescription. Next time,
you may bring your prescriptions to any of our
windows and the technicians will be happy
to fill them. Meanwhile, I'll suggest that our
signage is reassessed."

Listed below are suggested improvements for
anyone in the healthcare sector, organized
by Direct Patient Touch (tasks performed by
direct patient contact), Indirect Patient Touch

(tasks performed on behalf of the patient); and Media-related Patient Touch (tasks performed online and within the social media space).

Direct Patient Touch

1. Practice active listening
2. Assess the patient's body language
3. Comment in a nonjudgmental manner
4. Use simple, everyday language. Your patient is hearing what you are saying for the first time. Using medical jargon constructs a communication barrier.
5. Banish glib, condescending and disrespectful phrases from your vocabulary. Patients who ask follow-up questions should not be met with the response, "I do this for a living."
6. Educate patients on their conditions by having your Physician Assistant (PA) share hard copies of well-illustrated handouts with patients. The PA should sit beside the patient, not across from them, and help the

patient to understand their diagnosis and treatment.

7. Communicate on an equal footing. When in consultation with the patient, sit if the patient is seated.

8. Adjust your walking pace to that of the patient when leading him or her to an exam room. Walk beside the patient, not in front of them. Do not talk to the wall ahead of you while walking in front of the patient as he or she will not be able to hear you.

9. If you are a teaching physician ask the patient for permission to have a resident or intern accompany you while you assess the patient.

10. Provide a safe, pleasant and accommodating environment for the patient. Even if you are simply drawing blood and the patient experience lasts only five minutes, this, like every patient encounter, reflects on the ordering physician. Usually, blood draw areas are cramped, painted in uninviting colors

and devoid of a picture on the wall. As there is usually no hook on the back of the door to hang a coat, purse or cane, offer patients a safe place to store their belongings. Offer the same courtesy to caregivers who must carry the patients' belongings in addition to their own while blood is being drawn. Take an honest look at your lab. Is there a space to secure a walker or a wrist brace?

11. Communicate lab results and test results promptly by phone or online, then promptly mail a copy of the results to the patient or post them online. Do not make patients hunt you down for this information.

12. Make no assumptions about a patient's access to a computer, or cavalierly suggest that an 80 year-old "go online" to find more information about their diagnosis. Clear, informative, easy-to-read patient education materials are available through most medical associations.

Resist the temptation, if you are a Registered Pharmacist or a Licensed Pharmacy Technician, to staple the medication's information insert to the bag containing medication. Why? Because patients must examine the contents. Analyzing medical death rate data over an eight year period, Johns Hopkins[9] patient safety experts have calculated that more than 250,000 deaths per year are due to medical error in the U.S.[9]

When customers pick up medications, they should want to rip open the bag and verify this information:

A. Is this *my* prescription?
B. Is this the correct dose?
C. Is this how my prescription should look? For example, should the medication be a white, round tablet which is scored and has letters and numbers on it?

Only after this verification is complete should the Pharmacy Technician ask the customer, "Do you have any questions for the pharmacist?"

Indirect Patient Touch

1. Place 'Patient Complaints' on the agenda at all medical staff team meetings.
2. Don't punish patients by rushing them through their appointments when your schedule is backed up. Physicians who do this may cause their patients, who just arrived home, to ask themselves, "What just happened? Why did my medication get changed?" Just imagine the unsavory online reviews and phone calls to your office the next day.
3. Align your practice patterns with the emergent literature representing your discipline. This means extending the science that governs your specialty into the exam room, reception area and

waiting room. For example, if you are an orthopedic surgeon, do not expect older patients to be comfortable while waiting to see you if they must sit in chairs that are low to the ground.

4. Guard against new patients having to balance a series of forms on their laps without a clipboard, pen and adequate seating with which to complete such forms.

5. Do not cause unnecessary confusion and concern by sending a letter to every patient recommending that they repeat a test if a calibration error in a medical instrument impacted only a small subset of your patient population.

6. Reserve exam rooms that are close to the waiting room for those patients who have trouble walking.

7. See pharmaceutical reps either before or after seeing patients.

8. Replace germ-laden magazines with visually appealing, informative teaching

tools such as digital screens. These resources promote patient-provider communication and may also feature messages that reinforce your practice initiatives.

9. Question pharmacy design layouts. Why are pharmacists on raised platforms when they should speak to customers eyeball to eyeball? Similarly, while concern for privacy is critical, how can a petite woman at the 'Consultation' window be noticed when the tall steel-gray privacy partitions are larger than she? Wouldn't clear acrylic partitions maintain privacy and better allow her to be seen?

10. Sub-divide your clinic waiting room according to function. Patients should be greeted by staff whose sole purpose is to listen to and speak with patients, not answer the phone. Phone use should be managed in a separate area.

11. Proofread medication inserts carefully if you represent a drug manufacturer. For example, a drug insert informing patients of a side effect of their (external use only) ointment is 'metallic taste' does not inspire confidence in that manufacturer.

12. Produce medications that are not too big or too small. Imagine a senior with arthritis struggling to pick up a tiny pill in order to take it. Or worse, choking on a pill that is too large. Even cutting a pill in half can produce a rough edge that may irritate one's throat.

13. Remember that the customer picking up their medication may have just been diagnosed with a serious condition. Treat each customer you encounter or care for behind the scenes as you would your beloved parent.

14. Call your Call Center, pretend to be a patient, and gain insight into how your practice is being represented. Many large clinics outsource their Call Centers where patients

are not connected to the medical staff in the doctor's office, but to a remote location. This may place a barrier between doctor and patient. A remote call center may not know if the doctor has left for the day and cannot return a phone call. In addition, they may not know the contact information for a 'back-up' physician if needed.

15. Ensure that appointment reminders by phone clearly display your office name and number on your patients' caller ID systems. Do not take a chance that your patients mistake such calls as originating from scammers, resulting in their missed appointment and your ruined schedule. Patients should receive appointment reminders by phone within the hours of 9:00 a.m. and 5:00 p.m. unless otherwise arranged.

16. Design billing statements so that important information such as 'Date of Service' appears at the top along with other 'above the fold' information.

Assign all marketing messages and other non-billing related information to the bottom. This helps patients to reconcile their calendar ("Oh yes, that's when I had my CT scan.") and their checkbook. Additional billing statement recommendations follow:

A. Do not waste prime real estate at the top of the invoice by printing, 'Statement of Lab Services' or 'Laboratory Invoice' as the patient can readily see that the bill is from ABC123 Labs.

B. Do not print 'See Reverse Side for Important Information.' Important information belongs on the front of the bill.

C. Do not print the heading 'Statement of Professional Services' at the top of the bill. A bill from a physician does not need further explanation.

D. Reserve extraneous information for the back or bottom of the bill. Examples include payment plan information, return check fees, or thanks for choosing this healthcare provider.

17. Ask your spouse or a friend who is unfamiliar with the hospital or clinic where you work to accompany you there to view the flow of activity. Ask them:

    A. Is signage appropriately placed and clearly worded?

    B. Is there sufficient privacy of patient information provided through screens, partitions or separate rooms?

    C. Does staff appear to be friendly, helpful, informed and engaged?

    D. Are transport volunteers able to escort patients and visitors to each and every suite, lab, office or department?

18. Investigate the soothing value and comforting quality of certain colors and apply that research to your waiting room, exam rooms and clinics. There is no reason for a hospice room to be painted dark gray.

Media-related Patient Touch
Ensure that the website for your medical
supply organization has a search function. This
saves patients, caregivers and you time by
eliminating the need for phone calls asking, "I
know that you carry wrist braces. Do you carry
braces outfitted with a thumb splint which
might help with my carpal tunnel symptoms?"

5

IMPROVEMENTS FOR RETAIL

Success in the retail sector requires a focus on what matters to customers. That means helping them find what they are looking for, simplifying their purchasing process, and helping them check-out as soon as possible.

It *may* mean catering to the needs of an older woman who enters a lingerie store with a walker and asks an associate, "Do you have some beautiful teddies I can look at that would fit me on top *and* on the bottom?" Seniors want to be stylish, and have money to spend.

In his article, Joseph Coughlin maintains that the world's 65-plus population is the mother of all untapped markets.[10] It *always* means removing irritants so that a customers' experience is smooth and seamless. Here are more improvements for retail managers to consider:

Direct Customer Touch

1. Inform customers of their storm door delivery date, their garage door installation date, and when their car is ready to be picked up after it has been serviced.
2. Refrain from interrupting the customer who is complaining about a product or service. Interruptions most often occur because your organization's representative is assuming what your customer will say next. Allow the customer to vent before attempting to resolve the issue.

3. When speaking to customers, do not use jargon. Customers are hearing what you are saying for the first time.

4. Open as many cashier lines as you have available, with managers and other team members filling in as cashiers when there are long lines (of course, you have cross-trained all employees to function as cashiers when needed, right?). When I'm in a long cashier line I'll pull out my phone to call the store and ask them to open more registers. It works.

5. Be ready with directions when customers call to ask how to locate you. You and your employees commute to your store daily, yet when a customer loses their Global Positioning System (GPS) signal and calls your store for directions, too few employees know if your store is located east or west of Main Street.

6. If asked where a customer may find a product, escort the customer to that location. Do not point. Do not say, "It's

over there." "Do not say, "It's in the corner."

7. When speaking to customers, do not use jargon. For example, sale items are often placed at the 'end-cap' of an aisle. A retail team member shouldn't use this terminology with a customer however.

8. Eliminate the practice of making customers repeat their issue or experience with your product if they are transferred to another representative. The first representative should stay with the customer while transferring the customer to another representative, then repeat the customers' issue to the second representative, verify that the second representative can assist the customer, and only then should the first representative disengage with the customer.

9. Do not ask customers, "Did you find everything OK?" when they are checking out, as nothing can be done at this point.

Instead, install a call button in each department that customers can press that summons an associate.

10. Empower employees to use their best judgment.

11. Cross-train employees. Each associate behind the counter of the Customer Service Department should know how to transact each service within that department. For example, a Customer Service agent in a grocery store should be able to wire money, cash checks, handle bottle deposits, etc.

12. Ask yourself, "How can I help customers find what they are looking for faster?" Then ask yourself, "How can I help customers check-out faster?"

13. Exhibit effective listening. Too often, agents and representatives interrupt the caller because they assume that they know what the caller will say.

14. Respect customers' intelligence by backing up your claims. When a

customer arrives in your showroom to hear the 'superior sound quality' of your company's radio, be prepared with other radios on the market so that customers can compare the sound quality for themselves.

15. Look at each instance when you and your associates say "No" to customers and find a way to say, "Here's what we *can* do." Or say, "I know that you are disappointed. I'm sorry about that and I wish that we could do as you ask, but this is what I *can* do for you." This phrase expresses regret, displays empathy and makes the customer feel as if they have an option.

16. Take complaints seriously, and explain to customers exactly what happens to the suggestions that they offer you and your team members. Are they sent to the corporate office or managed locally? How often have you had a less-than-desirable retail experience and shared a

suggestion with a retail representative, only to have the representative murmur a lukewarm, "I'll let my manager know." Paying attention to customer complaints is your portal to learning about how you can delight your customers.

17. Explain the rationale behind your policy. Customers want to know the *why* and they chafe upon hearing, "It's store policy."

18. Ensure that each customer waiting in line can be easily seen by a cashier or representative that can assist them. Examine your waiting line model to assure that cashier and representative stations are positioned to face customers. Cashiers and representatives should not have their backs turned toward customers, necessitating the need to turn around to see if there is a customer waiting for service.

19. Identify with the customers' sense of urgency and forbid team members to gather and talk on the retail floor while

customers are waiting in line. To waiting customers, this is perceived as not placing customers' needs first.

20. Skip the music while customers are on hold. You will never arrive at a music genre or a volume setting that is pleasing to all. If you have placed a customer on hold, first explain the reason for doing so, and check-in while the customer is holding to assure the customer that they are not being abandoned.

21. Keep customers informed by sending them an automated response informing them that their email message was received and will be responded to within a set time period.

Indirect Customer Touch

1. Assign 'Customer Complaints' a priority position on the staff meeting agenda.

2. Ensure that you are not keeping callers on hold for five minutes or more while they are forced to listen to an on-hold

recording touting your 'rapid response' program.

3. Shortcut the time it takes for customers who call your company to be connected to the human being that can best assist them. Train phone representatives to say, "ABC Rentals, how may I help you?" instead of, "ABC Rentals, home of the free 10-pound bag of ice with each party package, this is Gloria."

4. Keep the price of sale items visible on store shelves until closing time on the last night of the sale. If the sale runs from Sunday through Saturday, and the store closes at midnight on Saturday, the sale price should still be visible on the shelves at 11:45 p.m. on Saturday. Prices for the new sale beginning on Sunday should be placed on store shelves after closing on Saturday or before the store opens on Sunday. You do not want a customer that expects to pay price 'A' see shelf price 'B' and leave without buying the item.

5. Empower your team members. If there is a register malfunction and the system isn't accepting a coupon, must a manager be summoned which will guarantee a longer line and frustrated customers?

6. Refrain from using 'advertainments' (exotic or character voices) in outgoing and on-hold messaging systems. Messages should be clear and easily understood.

7. Refrain from interrupting the customer who is complaining about a product or service. Allow the customer to vent before attempting to resolve the issue.

8. Train phone agents to manage the call to avoid time-consuming silence on both ends of the phone. What information is needed to assist the caller? If it is an account number, then ask for that. Do not ask customers to enter their account number using the touch pad on their phone, and then ask them to

repeat it when they are connected to an agent.

9. Re-examine the practice of sending a coupon for a free replacement product to a customer who complained about that product. Given the complaint, is it likely that the customer would want to use that same product again? Probably not. So why send a coupon for the same product? Instead, send a check to reimburse the customer for their cost.

10. Provide your organization's 800 number on the back of gift cards so that customers may check their balance at any time. The card giver may have opted not to disclose the amount.

11. Be consistent in the placement of sale items within your store. Position sale items at the front of the store, at the 'end cap' or end of the aisle, or at their regular place on the shelf. Your regular customers will remember your pattern, find their sale products easily, and not

waste their time in locating products. This practice also eliminates customers asking you where the sale products are, saving you time as well.

12. Provide separate floor space for different sizes. Petite and Ladies sizes each deserve their own floor space. Who wants to wade through the Ladies sizes to search for a Petite size?

13. Ensure that merchandise labels are intuitive. Imagine when shopping for men's large-sized socks, a customer saw nothing but a large 'M' on the label of each and every pair. He incorrectly assumed that the 'M' meant that the socks were medium-sized and left. He went to store #2 and looked at the rack of men's socks. There too, all the socks had the large 'M' and he assumed that they were medium-sized. He left and drove to store #3 where he asked a store associate to check and see if the socks came in large. Even the store

associate, after having searched for the desired size socks, emerged from the stock room and said, "I'm sorry but we only have the medium-size socks." Imagine the customer calling the manufacturer, whose number was on the label of the socks. He discovered that 'M' meant 'men's' not medium. He had traveled to three stores when he could have purchased the socks at the first store!

14. Pay your Customer Service (CS) and Customer Experience (CE) associates commensurate with the immense responsibility and authority assigned to them. These professionals are your links to company image and growth potential. They triage and untangle, educate and inform, quantify and resolve. Do not house them in the back room, in a basement, or at a remote location where they are separated from other company associates who have answers to the questions customers are

calling about. CS and CE associates are like loose diamonds deserving of the proper setting. They must be close to the decision makers, formulators and quality assurance staff. CS professionals deserve prominent placement in your organization. Your valuation of CS professionals is reflected through their salary and location within the organization.

15. Train technicians in cable companies to not leave a customer's home until the customer's issue has been resolved to the customer's satisfaction. Technicians should say to the customer, "You're all set now. Let's turn on your computer (or television) to make sure that you're connected."

16. Call your company from another phone and monitor the time it takes to connect to a human being.

17. Give all employees, old and new, a tour of the store to prepare them for when a customer asks them how to find

a product. How can your customers purchase a product if they can't find it?

18. Value existing customers by rewarding their loyalty. Too often, a promotional offer is restricted to new customers. Existing *and* new customers should enjoy a deal. Consider this hypothetical scenario. Many banks offer attractive promotions that are only available to new customers. After researching offers from competitive banks where a customer would be 'new' she withdrew money from her bank in person and then asked to see a bank officer. She announced to the officer that she was depositing her money in their competitor's bank because as an existing customer she was ineligible for the promotion. Bingo. She was offered an attractive promotion that met her needs on the spot.

19. Do not allow your organization's phone to ring more than three times before it is answered.

20. **Listen to your organization's outgoing messages.** You will enter the maze that customers find themselves in when they call your company. You may discover that there is no prompt ("Press one for billing.") for many issues. See for yourself how many customer concerns are missing an appropriate prompt. When is the last time you called your organization posing as a customer to ask a product-related question?

21. If your company's credit card carries a customer service phone number on the back of the card, ensure that the number is readable and not drowned out by the cardholder's credit card numbers that are embossed on the front. Check to see that your toll-free number is clearly shown without a number to letter conversion so that time isn't wasted searching the keypad for the right letters. Finally, ensure the readability of the 800-number itself.

Hint: Do not print white numbers on a light gray background.

22. Consider the packaging of your products. Arthritic fingers can't comfortably open and close pie or cake boxes outfitted with side flaps.

23. Train phone associates to use a script the same way good cooks use a recipe. That is, as a guide. Phone associates shouldn't sound like robots. Instead, they should enrich their calls by starting them with a smile, so that an easy conversation can be facilitated.

24. Hire Secret Shoppers® who pose as customers, use a company's products and services, and then report back to the company about their customer experience. Use Secret Shoppers® instead of asking customers to complete surveys. Customers who complete surveys rarely offer negative reviews, so the organizations that rely on surveys to tout their virtues are receiving and

using skewed data. Refrain from asking customers to contribute their time and perspective for free.

If you want customer feedback, hold focus groups and compensate participants accordingly. If you ask consumers to participate in a survey that would consume 15 minutes of their lives, are you placing the proper value on their time? Who among us can volunteer their time for a mere "Thanks for your feedback!" when these same volunteers will never get those 15 minutes back?

25. Schedule sufficient check-out personnel. It's not smart to make customers with money to spend in your store wait in line. If I'm waiting in a long line to check-out, I will call that same store and ask them to open another register. More often than not, it works. One line you won't find me in is the self-checkout lane. I do not supply free labor.

26. Re-program the cash register monitor data so that the sale price is displayed

when a sale product is scanned. Customers do not want to perform calculations, or struggle with new math while they are in line. They don't want to hear the cashier say, "The discount is applied at the end." The only price that the customer wants to see is the final sale price. That makes it easy for customers to check their receipts against the sale flyer.

27. Declutter the check-out area by clearing out magazines, lip balm and other items sold elsewhere in the store. A decluttered check-out counter offers more room for your employees to bag purchases, and more room for customers to place their purchases on the counter. Does anyone actually *buy* the items sold at the check-out counter?

28. Train your employees to keep their hands away from their mouths when they are speaking to customers, so that they are understood when speaking.

29. Practice economy of language in all platforms, for all audiences. Communicators and marketers should write to express, not to *im*press. Is your organization developing a new form? Give the draft to a neighbor or your mother. Can they understand how to complete it?

30. Change signs in restrooms from 'Employees Must Wash Hands' to 'Everyone Must Wash Hands' and ensure that there are adequate paper towels on hand or a hand dryer has been installed. I'm always amused when I enter a Ladies' Room that has hand dryers, not paper towels. Some hand dryers display elaborate (as many as six!) steps to follow for handwashing, describing the last step as "Take a paper towel and use it to open the door by the handle."

31. Decentralize the purchase of postage stamps by making them available at *all* registers. If stamps are only available at the Customer Service desk, customers

will need to wait in *two* lines. One for
groceries, and one for stamps.

32. Include an estimated wait time for your
    customers while they are on hold. Give
    them the option to remain on hold or
    request a call back without losing their
    place in line, or they will migrate to your
    competitor.

33. Ensure that the vendor of your cash
    register monitors installs them so that
    when the cashier says "Hello!" your
    customers can actually look the cashier
    in the eye while returning the greeting.

34. Be specific. A sign in a grocery store that
    reads "Fifty dollars feeds a family of four"
    is nonspecific, and leads the customer to
    think that they should donate fifty dollars
    toward the cause. A more effective sign
    would read, "Fifty dollars feeds a family of
    four. Give what you can."

35. Refrain from using zeros and the letter 'O'
    in all account numbers, form numbers,

etc. Nothing slows down the customer experience like being asked one's account number and not being sure if you are referring to letters or numbers.

36. Help consumers find you. Your online 'Directions' should identify at least two coordinating main streets on the map. Without context and coordinates, your customers are, literally, lost.

37. Avoid roadblocks that make coupon redemption impossible. It should not require a legal education to understand the language that is printed on a coupon.

38. Practice consistency. When I call a company to make a request and receive a 'No' from one representative, I call back and ask another representative the same question. I'm amazed at how often I receive a 'Yes' on the second try.

39. Cross-train your employees at all checkout lines.

There is no reason why, at appropriate times, a cashier at the online pick-up counter cannot check-out a customer purchasing in-store items.

40. Develop a failsafe way for customers to troubleshoot, so they may prevent a service call. For example, would it kill cable companies to color code cables and receptors so that a red cable gets inserted into a red hole?

41. Revisit all forms to ensure that they are intuitive and easy to complete. Well-designed forms do not require instructions. Users should be able to move through your form quickly and seamlessly. Before publishing any form, whether it is used in person or on your site, give it to an associate who does not interact with your department. Ask them to use their fresh eyes to test drive it, pointing out inconsistencies or anything that slows down its completion.

Do not ask for optional information on a form. Information is either required (necessary to include) or not required (and should be omitted). The form should be designed in a logical sequence, with similar questions grouped together, and with fields collected into logical groups. Prepopulate as much as you can for returning customers. Remember to be clear about input requirements. How often have you entered a username, not knowing that the system requires a number from one to nine as the first digit? Do not use zeros or the letter 'O' as these are indistinguishable from each other.

Media-related Touch

1. Don't ask for a consumer's name or email address when they are engaging in an online chat. Just answer the question.
2. Facilitate easy comparison shopping. If your organization sells tool sheds, enrich your site with a portable document

format (PDF) fact sheet for each tool shed model you carry. These PDFs can be downloaded, printed, spread out on a table, and evaluated using comparable specifications (dimensions, materials, warranty, delivery, etc.) to allow for easy comparison shopping, decision making and ordering.

3. Simplify the purchasing process for repeat online customers who expect that check-out screens be populated with as many fields as possible to save them time. You don't want a customer to leave your site because you did not remember them.

4. Do not advertise that walk-ins are welcome if, when a walk-in customer arrives, you ask her if she has checked in online. Walk-ins should do nothing more than (you guessed it!) walk in.

5. Stop insulting customers' intelligence by advertising that you offer 'Free Pick-up' at the store for products purchased online.

Customers are using *their* time and gas, not yours, to pick up the item.

6. Ensure that your site offers contact information in a conspicuous manner so that your customers can connect with you.

7. Don't expect customers to complete and submit a Contact Form only to wait for a response. Customers will move on to the next supplier that offers staff phone numbers and email addresses that enable questions to be answered quickly and easily.

8. Ensure that all site hyperlinks are working, especially on your organization's 'Contact Us' page. It's not good business to click on a hyperlink that reads, 'Send Us an Email' when clicking on it transports customers to an unrelated page.

9. Resist directing customers to your site via an on-hold message. If customers have taken the time to call you, they want to speak to a person.

10. Use built-in form validation if your
    site contains any forms for the user
    to complete so that required fields,
    minimum/maximum letters, and other
    parameters are specified and enable the
    validity of the form.

6

IS IT EASY FOR CUSTOMERS TO COMPLAIN TO YOU?

Just how easy is it for your customers to complain to your organization about its products, services and people? Do you invite constructive criticism or shun it? Is there a formal process for handling complaints? Has your site been thoroughly scrubbed of email addresses so that customers are prevented from contacting you? Or does your organization's leadership team openly invite feedback?

Certain organizations hold the highest standards of being transparent. They not only invite complaints, but explain exactly where a complaint should be sent. Like the elephant in the room, issues can only be resolved when they are brought to the surface and examined.

Remember our discussion about dissatisfied customers leaving your organization for your competitor and then complaining to their circle of friends about their negative experience?

Resolve now to invite complaints at each touchpoint in your customer's journey in these ways:

- Create a tab on your site entitled, "Got a complaint? Tell us about it."

Welcome feedback at each point in the customer's journey.

- Empower your team members to resolve customer complaints with the objective of retaining the customer.
- Contact customers after the sale using their preferred method of communication to glean information about how your product or service is performing.
- Attend to phone, site and written complaints, resolve the issue, then re-examine that touchpoint within the customer journey for possible process improvement.

7

FIRST-RATE EXPERIENCES

THIS CHAPTER RECOGNIZES CUSTOMER EXPERIENCES that I have found to be superior. I refer to them as improvements which are built from the ability to anticipate customer needs and the desire to fulfill them seamlessly.

Improved customer experiences are harvested from a sense of urgency, a display of empathy, and knowledge about your line of products and services. Anyone possessing these qualities is a true ambassador of improved customer experiences.

These improvements delight customers, enrich their customer experience, and make them want to return to that organization again and again. They are reproducible by every employee, in every business, and in every business sector.

Improvement Examples:

1. At a deli counter, a clerk sliced a pound of ham for me. Her colleague noticed that no other customers were waiting, and asked me if I needed anything else from the deli so that while my ham was being sliced, he could fulfill the other items on my list.
2. I called a company that manufactures compression gloves to ask if the gloves ease the symptoms of carpal tunnel syndrome, namely pain and swelling. The person that answered the phone actually knew the product line so well that she promptly answered my question, and

masterfully so, without transferring me to someone else.

3. My friend required a series of vitamin B12 injections. She worked nights at the time, and required late afternoon appointments. At the end of the first injection appointment, the nurse gave her a calendar sheet pre-populated with all future injection appointments that accommodated her schedule, so that my friend did not need to arrange any future appointments.

4. I ordered two large meat and cheese trays for a party I hosted. When I arrived to pick up the trays, I learned that they had not been prepared, and I expected 30 guests at my door in two hours! The deli associate asked me for the address of the party. She said that the manager would deliver the trays himself. He arrived as promised. In addition to the two meat and cheese trays, a tray of shrimp with cocktail sauce appeared with

his compliments. He also presented me with a flower arrangement for the party, and a gift card to use at the store, in an effort to invite me back. I *did* return to that store.

5. I purchased a pair of men's cufflinks from a jeweler, and requested that they be monogrammed. Before picking them up, I checked the jeweler's site to discover when they were closing. The site posted an 8:00 p.m. closing time. It was only 6:45 p.m. so I had plenty of time. When I arrived at the jeweler, I discovered that it closed at 7:00 p.m. I called the jeweler the next day and explained my experience. It appears that the jeweler was a victim in this instance. Many sites reflect incorrect opening and closing times, so it is best to call the store. As an effort to win back my business, the jeweler absorbed the cost of the monogramming, and I was presented with a lovely gift.

NOTES

1. Lateef, Fatimah. "Patient expectations and the paradigm shift of care in emergency medicine." Journal of Emergencies, Trauma and Shock. (April-June, 2011):163-167.
2. Newman, Daniel. "Customer Experience is the Future of Marketing." *Forbes*. October 13, 2018. Forbes.com. https://www.forbes.com/sites/danielnewman/2015/10/13/customer-experience-is-the-future-of-marketing/#5f2cd990193d
3. Closing the delivery gap: How to achieve true customer-led growth. Bain & Company. James Allen, Frederick F. Reichheld, Barney Hamilton and Rob Markey. October 5, 2005. Bain.com/insights/closing-the-delivery-gap-newsletter/

4. Dixon, Matthew, Nick Tonan and Rick Delisi. *The Effortless Experience: Conquering the New Battleground for Customer Loyalty.* Portfolio. 2013.
5. Rogers, Charlotte. Consumers Will Spend More on Simple Brand Experiences. *Marketing Week.* February 3, 2017.
6. Siegel+Gale. "Siegel+Gale Unveils Seventh Annual Global Brand Simplicity Index."™ Siegel+Gale press release, January 25, 2017.
7. Spenner, Patrick and Karen Freeman. "To Keep Your Customers, Keep it Simple." *Harvard Business Review.* May, 2012.
8. Triage. *Merriam-Webster.com Dictionary, Merriam-Webster,* https://www.merriam-webster.com/dictionary/triage. Accessed 22 Aug. 2020.
9. McMans, Vanessa. "Johns Hopkins Study Suggests Medical Errors are Third-Leading Cause of Death in the U.S." *The BMJ.* May 3, 2016.
10. Coughlin, Joseph F. "The Longevity Economy: Why Seniors Are a Fast-Growing Emerging Market." *Barron's,* December 7, 2018.

ACKNOWLEDGMENTS

When one has a sibling, they are considered blessed. I have three. Thank you to my amazing brothers, Vincent, Carl and David Gargano. Their eternal "Go for it!" encouragement enriched my life.

I owe special thanks to Carl Gargano and Danny T. Burns. Their meaningful suggestions made this a better book.

Deep gratitude goes to Adrienne B. Naumann, J.D., for her expert legal review of the manuscript. Adrienne, you are the maven. Special recognition goes to Yvonne Dixon, Fellow of the Society of Indexers, who saw the big picture of the book and distilled the concepts into indexable terms.

ABOUT THE AUTHOR

Theresa has assisted firms of all sizes in an array of industries. She has worked with Fortune 100 companies to create strategic marketing programs and provide thought leadership for a range of mid-sized firms. She is a recipient of the 'Above and Beyond the Call of Duty' award for her work at Kraft Foods. As a consultant with Alliant Foodservice Inc., she repositioned a suite of publications and managed an employee communications program that won an APEX award for publication excellence.

Theresa has a master's degree in Institutional Management and a master's degree in Business Administration. She is listed in *Who's Who of American Women*.

INDEX

www.ingramcontent.com/pod-product-compliance
Lightning Source LLC
Chambersburg PA
CBHW022045190326
41520CB00008B/709